ATMASWARUPAM
One's Own Real Nature

ATMASWARUPAM
One's Own Real Nature

SRI ADWAYANANDA
–Sri K. Padmanabha Menon–

Talks video-recorded
by the National Centre for the Performing Arts, India,
for its archives

ADVAITA PUBLISHERS
1988

Library of Congress Catalog Card No. 88-70938.
ISBN 0-914793-15-2

For information, address the Publisher: Sri Vidya Samiti, Malakara via Chengannur, Kerala State, India, or Advaita Publishers, P.O. Box 5046, Austin, Texas 78763, U.S.A.

Preface

As some people asked for a transcript of the video recording of these talks, to make it easily available to them, this has been published in book form. Here, some of the basic questions are asked and answered.

KPadmanatha menon

INTRODUCTION
(As Presented on the Video Recording)

The National Centre for the Performing Arts is concerned with the preservation and development of the total spiritual and cultural legacy of India. It is just as important for the Centre to record the Spiritual teachings as to record the artistic and cultural teachings and traditions.

Truly speaking it is not possible to record the Guru because He can be recorded only in the heart. Nevertheless an attempt has been made, with the means available, to record the talks of a great Guru of South India, Sri K. Padmanabha Menon, in an attempt to preserve for posterity what He expounds.

Born in Kerala, Sri K. Padmanabha Menon (Sri Adwayananda) is the elder son and disciple of the great Sage Sri Krishna Menon (Sri Atmananda), who was Himself a householder and a responsible officer in Government Service.

In 1966, seven years after Sri Gurunathan's Mahasamadhi, Sri Gurudev came out, to fulfill the needs of those who came to Him seeking spiritual guidance and enlightenment.

It is noteworthy and interesting that we have here a succession of householder Gurus not removed from life in the ordinary sense.

The National Centre is privileged to have been able to record the talks of this great Sage.

Sri Jamshed J. Bhabha, Chairman,
National Centre for the
Performing Arts, India

RECORDED TALKS

MORNING TALK

Questioner: I have been asked how it is relevant for the archival recording which the National Centre for the Performing Arts is doing of all the arts which depend on oral tradition—principally music, which depends on the *Gurukula* system—how is it relevant to also record oral Spiritual teaching, as we are doing today?

Gurudev: It is rather difficult, but still, it is from that only that all the other arts, even the oral teaching in the other arts, can exist. The background must be this, because all these arts take you to this Centre. Otherwise, the music has—music or painting or whatever art you have, dancing—all these arts have no strong basis. In fact, I don't know in other languages, in Sanskrit or in Malayalam the word for "art" is *kalā*. "Ka" refers to *Brahma*. So, any art must take you—Indian art, especially, takes you—to This. That is the real background of all the Indian arts.

Questioner: *Kalā?*

Gurudev: *Kalā.* "Ka" refers to *Brahma,* that letter. So the real oral teaching, the Spiritual, it may be difficult to be recorded, but still . . . It can be only in the oral teaching—the real enlightenment. So it is not, you cannot call it even, teaching. It is actual Seeing and that is possible only in the world between the real, earnest disciple and the right, living Guru, where there is no duality. There is no giving, no taking. It is pure Experience. And that is possible only in this world between the Guru and the disciple. That is rather difficult to be recorded. But still, as much as possible . . .

Questioner: How does that real culture reach one through art, theatre, dance? In what way is he in contact with this Spirituality?

Gurudev: You see, if he develops further in his art, then one day he is sure to reach this. There is one example we have—Tyagaraja. He rose to the Spiritual through music. If rightly directed, guided, they can reach that. That—the expression, the sound—*Nāda Brahma,* they call it, you reach that. And reach that silent music which is pure Experience itself. And only that, within, can produce beautiful outward expression. This expression will take you to the expressed, and that expressed is the pure Experience. Art has its real basis or value here. One day or other one is sure to reach it. Without that, however much you may play, it will not take you far. But there is certain music—when you listen you can see you are transported somewhere that you yourself may not know where you are taken.

Questioner: That may be in music. But what about painting or dancing?

Gurudev: In the same way. As I said, the expression takes you to the Expressed, which you cannot define. Haven't you heard that there is music in painting? I think UNESCO has published a book like that: *Music in Painting*. So they are all one, in the right . . . way.

Questioner: I would like to ask the question: Why was I born? What is the meaning of life? What will happen after I die? I want to know the meaning of life.

Gurudev: First you want to know why you are born? And what, what is your position after death?

Questioner: I want to know that, and the meaning of life.

Gurudev: Yes. First you have to know, what do you mean by being born? Who is born? And who is dying? If you know *that* first, then birth and death you can more or less understand. When you are—when you say that you are born and you die, that itself shows that you have a stand beyond these: birth and death. Essentially you are That. That is never born. That is never going to die. And birth and death are only in the body level. There is a false identification in the level of the body and mind, and you say you are that, the embodied I. It is that which is born and which is dying. You stand beyond that. For That, there is no birth, no death. And you will be asking: what is the meaning of life? Really you find the meaning of life only in the Spiritual. During your life, if you examine all your activities, you will see either you want happiness or knowledge, only in this way. You may be doing many things, but still, the sole aim of all these activities is—is only this. And here only you get the real meaning of your life. And till you get there at least for a short time, you won't be satisfied. You want either happiness or knowledge. Both are one in that level of Experience. Knowingly or unknowingly, you are only seeking this. Here only you find the real meaning. Whatever other things you are doing, you are not satisfied *till* you come to this point. You want further clarification about this? Am I elaborate enough? Or do you want further . . . ?

Questioner: Is that the reason why people keep constantly changing the objects in their lives?

Gurudev: That is only because they think that the objects will bring them happiness. So they first go to one object, and then after some time that is not enough. They want to go to another object. And a third time they want, still want to go to another. Like that, they go on changing object after object. Still their pursuit is after happiness. If the happiness was there in the object—the first object they went to—there was no need for them to change it. So that clearly shows the objects do not contain happiness. Does the mind contain happiness? If the mind had it, then there was no need for anyone to go to that object. So it is not even in the mind. But when the desired object is got, you enjoyed happiness. How was it possible? There is no happiness in the mind, there is no happiness in the object. But when you got the desired object, you enjoyed happiness—that is a fact. That you cannot deny. How is it possible then? What happened is: when you were desiring the object, your mind was restless, and when you got the desired object, this restlessness stopped, and you are able to take note of your Real Nature which is Happiness itself. This is what happens here. But this you wrongly take that you got it from the object.

What was your question then? What was your question? Is it enough?

Questioner: Then the aim of my life, of anyone's life, should be . . .

Gurudev: To reach Yourself.

Questioner: . . . is to reach . . .

Gurudev: Yourself.

Questioner: Himself.

Gurudev: Yes. In fact, anybody in the world is knowingly or unknowingly seeking Self-realisation.

Questioner: That is then the aim of anybody's life.

Gurudev: Yes, but if you say that to anybody in the world, they may not admit it. But if you carefully examine, you will see that is the only thing that they are aiming at. They want happiness, they want knowledge. They want to be permanent: that is the changeless aspect. They want to be free. Anything you seek, when you examine, you will see that you are only seeking your own real Self. That means Self-realisation. Even unknowingly, anybody—even a criminal—is only seeking this. He thinks by doing this criminal act he will, at least for the moment, he will reach this. But once you know the right path, one will not turn to this wrong . . . path, choose this wrong path. He will follow the right line, and reach his destination.

Questioner: But how can I achieve Self-realisation, how can I come to it?

Gurudev: Self-realisation? When the urge is strong enough, you will come to the right line.

Questioner: Through the Guru?

Gurudev: Yes, the Guru will come. Or you will find

the proper Guru when the strength, when the urge is strong. When you are earnest.

Questioner: Without the Guru it cannot be achieved?

Gurudev: Impossible. Generally that is what our Spiritual history teaches us.

Questioner: Why is that?

Gurudev: Because you will get involved again. In the process of activity you will get involved again in the body-mind identification. There, there must be Somebody who has gone beyond that, to put you beyond that. Even Shankara had His Guru and what He said is, *Deshi-koktyā Shivoham* ("I am the Absolute through the words of my Guru").

Questioner: How is one self related to another self?

Gurudev: You mean in the ordinary . . . ?

Questioner: You have a gathering of people. They are all seeking Self-realisation. What is the relationship between one self and another self?

Gurudev: Two people seeking the real . . . ? It is only through that. That is the real relationship. The one man—one man is seeking the Reality, the other man is seeking the Reality. That is the real relationship between two people. Any other relationship will naturally fall, because finally you will come to this. This is the *lasting* relationship, if at all you speak of relationship. And you are speaking of the relationship of the disciple to the Guru, also it is almost like that. Because the Guru—it will not be possible through the mind to reach this level.

There is a—there is another faculty called the Higher Reason or, in Sanskrit, we call *Vidyā*. It is through that the Guru speaks. From that, from His level, the Guru speaks. And this *Vidyā* aspect will be automatically awakened in the listener when the urge is there and he is listening. And it is through that he is following and then the disciple reaches that level from where the Guru is speaking. He gets the real Experience, seeing the Truth. At that point there is neither Guru nor disciple. Only if like this—only the real Guru can take the disciple to this, where there can be neither Guru nor disciple.

And I said *Vidyā* aspect. There is another way of putting it. The Truth cannot be shown by anything else, because Truth is unity. Truth can be shown only by Truth itself. But how can we understand this? That is why Teachers have said: Truth has two aspects—the passive principle and the active principle. It is said it is through the active principle that you reach the passive. Why active principle, it is said? There is a seemingly active part of it: the Guru speaks, the disciple listens and follows. So there is a seeming activity there. There is no— there is not a mental understanding. It is not—nothing like that. But there is a seeming activity there. It is through this active principle that you reach the passive principle, and when you reach that point, there is neither the passive nor active. It is there that you get the real Experience—the real Seeing.

Questioner: When you reach that point where there is neither the active nor the passive . . .

Gurudev: It is the real Experience.

Questioner: It is pure Experience?

Gurudev: Pure Experience.

Questioner: Being?

Gurudev: Yes.

Questioner: I am? All of that?

Gurudev: Not even that, just—pure Light.

Questioner: Pure Light.

Gurudev: Yes. There is nobody who sees the Light, there is nobody who gives the Light, nothing. Pure Experience. That is unity. It is there that the real Advaitic teaching takes you. Advaitic, "non-dual." It is unity, that is one. All the diversity leads you only here, to this.

Questioner: How can people in the world find the Guru?

Gurudev: If there is that earnestness and urge, they will surely find. It is a part of their seeking. If that seeking is earnest and sincere, surely the seeker will go to the right person. There can be a question: how can you know that you have gone to the right person? But this is the criterion: if their earnestness—if there is that earnestness, if the urge is strong, he will surely go to the right person. Otherwise he won't be satisfied by going to this man or that man. Generally such seekers are rare. Few, at least, let us say in the minority. And the Gurus also are rare.

Questioner: It is said that there are two kinds of Gurus: the *kārya guru* . . .

Gurudev: And *Karana Guru*. *Kārya guru* is one who has reached up to a certain point and who can take the disciple up to the point he has reached. *Kārana Guru* is one who has reached the Absolute, and He will be in a position, He will be able, to take the seeker or the disciple to the Absolute itself. And there is Shankara's verse:

Drishtānto naiva drishtas tribhuvanajathare
sadguror jnānadātuh
sparshash cettatra kalpyah sa nayati yadaho
svarnatām ashmasāram
na sparshatvam tathāpi shritacharanayuge
sadguruh svīyashishye
svīyam sāmyam vidhatte bhavati nirupamas
tena cā'laukiko'pi

(Nothing in the world can be compared to the Guru who gives the Highest Knowledge.

The philosopher's stone (*sparsha*) converts any base metal into gold; whereas the Sat Guru makes His disciple, who has surrendered to His Feet, identical to Himself.

Therefore, the Sat Guru is incomparable.)

So nothing can be compared with the Guru. And *that* world which exists between the Guru and the disciple— the real world, I told you that there is neither the Guru nor the disciple at the Real—that world between the Guru and the disciple is the *real basic culture* of India.

Questioner: To follow the Guru, is there a necessity to renounce the world, to become as a monk or a *sanyāsin?*

Gurudev: You are not—. The Truth is in spite of anything. So if it exists in spite of anything, to reach that also it is, it must be, in spite of anything. So what is there to renounce if the world is used in its intrinsic merit of showing This only? There is no question of renunciation.

Questioner: How is it that the world can be used to help me there, to go towards Self-realisation?

Gurudev: What is reality?

Questioner: The Truth.

Gurudev: What is that? In Sanskrit we call it *Sat*, *Chit*, and *Ānanda*. That is from this side. You have your life, thought, and feeling. And it is from this level we call it *Sat*, *Chit*, and *Ānanda*. In that level it is one, pure Experience.

What is *Sat*? You call it *Sat* because it is changeless. How do you say that it is changeless? Because you are able to take notice of the changes in the world, including that of your body and mind. That shows you are beyond the body and you are changeless. Only if you are changeless you can notice the changes, otherwise you won't be able to notice the changes. That is why it is called *Sat*.

Then there is the knowledge. What is knowledge? Knowledge *of* something is not knowledge. It is only a thought. Knowledge is pure Experience. Knowledge has nothing to know. It is not even a function . . . You see, when you say, "I see this object," already the knowing is over. It is only a thought. At the moment when you say you see the object, it is only a thought. Then if the knowing is over, at the moment of exact knowing, what was your position? Pure Knowledge. And that is Experience. So, at that moment, you are in your own Self, the Reality, pure Knowledge.

Then there is that Bliss, or Happiness. I have said a few minutes ago that there is no object which can give you happiness. Still you are seeking happiness through objects, changing one object after another. The mind also does not contain happiness. Then how do you get your happiness? The mind does not contain happiness, the object does not contain happiness. How is it that when

14

you get the desired object you enjoy happiness? I told you that when you are desiring an object, the mind is restless, and when you get the desired object, the mind has come to rest. At that moment you are able to notice your real nature which is Happiness itself.

So, there are three aspects, so to say, from this side. Changeless aspect—that is *Sat*. Knowledge or Consciousness—*Chit*. And Happiness, Bliss, Peace, or Love—*Ānanda*. They are all one in that level of pure Experience. This is the nature of the Reality, or the Real "I." The Real "I" is this. What was your question?

Questioner: How can the world, the objects in the world, take me to that?

Gurudev: Yes. Now, if there is an object, how do you say that there is an object? Because you know it, is it not?

Questioner: Yes.

Gurudev: So the object only points to Knowledge. It shows That. So any object is only a thought form, which only directs you towards That. Instead of getting stuck up in that way, if you turn to the direction it points to, you are at the right point.

Questioner: But what about feelings?

Gurudev: Feeling is also like that. Feeling also points to Happiness.

15

Questioner: But then there are negative feelings.

Gurudev: Negative feelings. But even the negative feelings only point to the positive. Without a reference to the positive there cannot be a negative existence for feelings. Any feeling, if you examine, you will see the basis is love. Love: the basis. "I am the Light of Consciousness in all thoughts and perceptions and the Light of Love in all feelings" (*Ātmā Darshan*)—any feeling, negative or positive. The basis is that. Love. Love is Truth itself. When you examine any negative feeling, you will see that it is only a wave in This.

Questioner: I am sorry, Gurudev, but I don't see how a negative feeling . . .

Gurudev: Take the example of a negative feeling.

Questioner: Anger.

Gurudev: Anger. What is it, what is that anger? You get angry here, at this moment, with somebody. Is it not because you expect something else from him?

Questioner: Yes.

Gurudev: So, is not the Love in that expressed as anger here? That is not found here, so you get angry. So this, this expression is only in reference to That. That Love. Is it not? So how can anger be there, when you see this? Any negative feeling, if you examine, you will see

16

that it is only like this. Anger, sorrow, anxiety—all this, when you examine it rightly, you will see that it has always that direct reference to the positive feeling, Love, the positive basis, Love. It is to take you to this that all these exist. If you can see that, then you are safe. You are, you can never be disturbed by anything. In a poetic way my Father spoke in *Ātmā Nirvriti*. There is a chapter called "Atma's Disappointment." Atma cannot be disappointed, but He has put it in a poetic way, that is all: "I created thoughts, feelings, perceptions and the rest as a means whereby I could make Myself known. . . . I created a deep-sleep state; it was also meant to make Myself known"—because in deep-sleep there is no object, but you have the peace and knowledge. So whatever you have in this world, rightly understood or rightly seen, will only help you here.

Questioner: May I? Can it be said that the real culture of India comes from the relationship between the Guru and the disciple?

Gurudev: Any culture must lead you to find the complete answer to what you are seeking, knowingly or unknowingly. It is here any culture is guiding you. It is on that the whole thing, all this, is conveyed, is it not? Without this, is there a peace? So, is it not based on that? Can it come from any other basis? You may say "peace." What is peace? You may say "happiness." What is happiness? You may say "knowledge." What is knowledge?

When you want to come to this, only in *this* way you can open your eyes.

Questioner: But culture would generally . . .

Gurudev: Any culture is based on this.

Questioner: We speak about the Guru-disciple relationship, but not everybody can avail himself of such a relationship.

Gurudev: I told you, an earnest seeker will find.

Questioner: But there are many scriptures which have been written. How can they help the average man that is seeking from a different level?

Gurudev: Levels may be different but the search is the same. Scriptures are all right to read, but you must not get stuck up there. And if there is no discrimination in reading, that also can in a way sometimes cause impediments. There are three *vāsanas* which are supposed to be impediments to Spiritual realisation. One is *deha-vāsana*—that means *vāsanas*, tendencies, connected with the body. The second is *loka-vāsana*—tendencies connected with the world. How, what, is the world? How is this, how is that—like that, that tendency. The third is scriptures—*shāstra-vāsana*. One can get stuck up there also. That also is an impediment. It is not enough if you read scriptures and learn by heart or interpret and become a scholar, that is not enough. And if you develop a tendency in that, that itself can be an impediment sometimes. And it is said also that you must read according to directions from the proper person. Otherwise there is a possibility of getting confused.

Questioner: We spoke about *kalā*.

Gurudev: Yes.

Questioner: Is there any similar root origin in Sanskrit for music or beauty?

Gurudev: Beauty is—I don't know, they say *saundarya* is the word for it. But real *saundarya* or beauty cannot be defined. There is beauty in music, there is beauty in poetry, beauty in forms, scenery and all that. But what is this? You cannot define. Beauty is the real Experience. But when you say, "beautiful," you come down to the level of object. But the beauty in all this is one—the pure Experience. You cannot define it. The real beauty you find . . . you reach the real beauty through all this.

In fact, there is in man these three tendencies: the tendency towards beauty, the tendency towards wonder—sense of wonder there is in any man—and the sweetness. We cannot define what is sweetness. We cannot define what is beauty. We cannot define what is wonder. These are there, but these tendencies get fulfilled only at the Absolute. Nowhere else. You will be seeking

19

here and there, but what is sweetness? Sugar is not sweet. That sweetness is not sweetness. There is something deeper than that—that *rasa* which is the basis, the basis of all this. That is the real sweetness. There is a sense of wonder, but what is that? You can't define. But that is also fulfilled only at this level. And there is that beauty. What is beauty? You can say, "This is beautiful, that is beautiful," but what is beauty? It is pure Experience. That is how, maybe unknowingly, Keats said: "Beauty is truth, truth beauty."

Questioner: Do the scriptures throw any light on the past, present, and future, which are very important in Western thinking? Past, present, and future—the meaning of those terms? Future, what is the future in relation to the past?

Gurudev: In a way you can say the past produces the present, and the present shows the way to the future. But these are all in the level of time. Time we have to know also. But we cannot just put the emphasis on the object level only. There, the time element comes. When you examine correctly, you will see you can have only one thought at a time. And that thought merges or disappears, and then you come to the next thought. What is there to connect these two thoughts? Really, when one thought is there, you stand as the Witness. That is how you say, you are able to say that there is a thought—and, after that has finished, the second thought. And in between, it is the Reality itself. But because of the usual practice, whenever you think of "I," you think of the embodied "I." And because of that you put the embodied "I" in the place of the Witness, which is the Reality. And when you put in the embodied self, you *claim* the thought. It is then that you say, "I have the thought." Otherwise, thought is witnessed.

Witnessing is *not* a function. It is the quality of Reality. Just as the sun lights the world: it is not the function of the sun, it is just the quality of the sun. Like that, the Reality comes as the Witness when you think that there is a thought, when you have, consider, that there is a thought. And when that thought has merged, you have another thought. In between is pure Consciousness or the Reality. But when you put the embodied self there, then you connect the thoughts, as yesterday, today, and tomorrow.

When instead of one thought—when you imagine that there can be more than one—it is then, at that point, the idea of time comes in. Just as you take the example of the sun. Sun rises—sets. The rising sun is one thought. The setting sun is another thought. They are two independent thoughts. There is nothing to connect. But when you think that there is the embodied self to connect, it is then that you say the rising sun sets. Otherwise, rising sun never sets. They are two different thoughts.

And if they are two different thoughts, where is the time that is coming in—twelve hours—between these? Where is the time? So, if the rising sun never sets, the twelve hours do not come in there. They are two independent thoughts. That is how the time element comes: when instead of one thought, when you imagine that there is more than one thought. It is there that the time element comes in. "I see this." When the embodied self is put in the place of the Witness: "I saw this yesterday, I see this now." Memory also comes in only here. So the two thoughts are connected. Otherwise, one thought has occurred, and it has merged, and the second thought comes. There is no connection. Only when this is connected, when the thoughts are connected like this—the time element comes in. Only then there is the past, present, and future.

And so many thoughts or ideas put together you call space. Because of one thought preceding and the other following, causality comes. Time, space, and causality— on these, the world exists. Only on *this* basis can you speak of the past, present, and future. If this is seen, connections fall and the right Seeing comes. If time, space, and causality are explained and Truth shown by the living *Kārana Guru*, the world stands answered. It removes all doubts, and the Truth established automatically.

Questioner: What is this Witness?

22

Gurudev: Witness is pure Consciousness itself. When there is a thought, it is recorded there. Just as I told you, the sun lights all the objects of the world. It is not a function of the sun. It is a quality. That is all. It is because of the Witness that you say you have a thought. Any object is a thought. When you recognise an object, it is as: "I see the object." It is only a thought. And then pure Consciousness becomes the Witness there.

Questioner: It is not a function?

Gurudev: No. Witnessing is not a function. It is only a superimposition on pure Consciousness.

Questioner: What is the nature of the link between the body and the mind and the higher Self which You have been talking about? How is it important to maintain the health of the body, and how is it that the finest being can be destroyed by a terrible infection which may affect the mind, like meningitis, that destroys all the central faculties and Spiritual capacities and everything?

Gurudev: The real Spiritual level can *never* be destroyed by anything. The body and mind are only seen. We can see the body's activities, the body's developments. Similarly, the mind's activities, the mind's developments. You stand beyond this, and it is because of that that you are able to see the changes which are taking place in the body and mind. And you *never* undergo any change. Only then you are happy. This cannot be destroyed. What is destruction there? You—when You stand beyond even destruction—then where is the destruction? What destruction? About what?

Questioner: No, the question is: the health of the mind is affected by the health of the body. That is the question. When the body is in disrepair, the mind in its functions gets in disrepair.

Gurudev: It can be just the other way also. When the mind is healthy, the body can be healthy also.

Questioner: What about infection like meningitis which is not something caused by psychology?

Gurudev: Yes. Something like that may be. But generally when the mind is healthy, they say the body also can be generally healthy. Because, what they say, even the doctors say, if you eat when you are happy, the food is better assimilated than when you are anxious or worried. So, the mind's health helps a lot towards the health of the body, and the mind can be healthy if it is, if you stand, beyond that. The stand is there. You are always at Peace and when you are at Peace, the mind is not disturbed. And you can keep the stand only by awakening to the Higher, to the real "I," which is Yourself.

Questioner: Could You repeat what You said once about when the dance begins? You were saying . . .

Gurudev: Yes, it begins with the worship . . . When a musician starts, he always starts with a song in praise of some god—Ganapati or Ganesh or Saraswati, like that. Same is the case with the dancer also. He also begins the performance with a sort of worship. So far as India is concerned, all the arts are like this. They have unknowingly that direction towards that. But all the performers may not be realising that. If you recognise that, art will be better developed also.

AFTERNOON TALK

Questioner: Dr. Radhakrishnan, in his book, *Philosophy of Vedanta*, wrote that the individual desires to live more, and still more, and surpass himself in order to reach fullness of being. Dr. Radhakrishnan is no more with us. The individuals who are with You now and from time to time, Your disciples or seekers of the Truth, seek guidance on similar themes. What is the individual in terms of a starting point and end point—life and death? And what is the kind of fullness of being, or satisfaction in life, which You could guide the seekers of Truth and disciples to find?

Gurudev: All these tendencies come from within because really or essentially, you are perfect and full. And it is from *There* that you get this tendency to become full, to become perfect, to develop, not wanting to die: because really you are—the real "I" is—beyond birth and death. It is from There all these tendencies come down to mankind. A man wants perfection. The perfection is achieved only at that, at the Ultimate, because it *is* perfection itself. So he has a tendency to become perfect, and because he is in the embodied level, he tries to bring all this, to achieve all this, from this level. Really one cannot become perfect in this. The only thing one has to do is to remove that veil which blocks this perfection which is Himself, the Reality. And that is the false identification with the body and mind. And it is this that you call "I" in the ordinary level of life. If that ego, this false identification is removed, which is the main—which is *the*—veil which blocks the sight, then everything that you seek is achieved. Any more elucidation or explanation needed there, in this?

And this is the real Spiritual achievement. The search, when one turns to the Spiritual, it is There that he gets the fulfilment and the answer to all this. That is why I said the whole phenomenal life finds its meaning only in the Spiritual. Otherwise you don't know why you are doing this, why you are doing that—it goes on indefinitely. Nobody asks you: "You must do this." What for? When you examine it correctly, in the right perspective, you will see that you are only seeking this. As I said this morning, anybody in the world is only seeking Self-realisation. Whatever you may say—perfection, fullness, all this—where do you find it? Here only, in this realisation of the Self. There—it is from There that these tendencies come down to you and you want to achieve it in this level. That is your work. The whole work is only for That.

Questioner: But for the individual the self is expressed in terms of the individual drives, desires . . .

Gurudev: Yes.

Questioner: . . . longings, cravings.

Gurudev: When they are rightly examined you can see that they are all there only to show you This, and only there you find answers to all this. You don't want to die—but the Reality is always. If it begins at a certain time and ends in another time, it is not Reality. That is your real Self, and it is because of that that you never want to die, end your life. You don't like it.

Questioner: In which case, what is the cycle of the body—birth and death?

Gurudev: Yes, that is according to the theory—there is a reincarnation theory—that is, whenever you do something, when you claim the action, there is a doer. And because of the doer that action leaves—action, thought, or feeling leaves—a residue in you. That is what you call the *samskāras*. These *samskāras* are there in you, in your subconscious state. And according to the main *samskāras*, or the sum total of all this, you choose the next body to develop these. Till you come to a level that you are no more the doer. Really, there is no doer of

29

an action. Only *after* the action the doer is introduced. And then the claiming comes: "I did that," "I had this thought," "I had this feeling"—like that. So when once you see the Truth—that there is no doer, no enjoyer, no perceiver—these *samskāras* stop. And once the *samskāras* stop, the cycle also stops. Then you are at the right spot. It is towards that anybody is striving.

Questioner: Why are some people born more advantageously than other people?

Gurudev: Does this not give answer to that? According to one's own actions. From this level we see: "Oh, some people are more advantageously born, others are not." But it depends . . . it is according to his *karmas*, or that man's *karma*, that he is born. Though from this level, or from this point of view, we may see there is this difference. It is because of this that there are differences. However much you may try to make them equal, the *karmas* remain. That does not mean that you must not make any effort to give good opportunities to all. That is all right. But still the real answer is here.

Questioner: It was just said that the false identification with the body and mind is something like a veil which covers the Truth. But is it possible to live without being identified at all with the body and mind?

Gurudev: What is life? What is life?

Questioner: Generally we think of . . .

Gurudev: What is life? As I said, even without your knowing, you are making use of life towards this.

Questioner: But there is still something on that side.

Gurudev: Yes, it is towards That. And when this aim is kept, that is the life. So the whole life becomes a meditation towards this. So can you take into account the false identification there? When this aim is clear, where is the question of identification? The whole life becomes a meditation. I can quote one of Shankara's verses in this context. It is difficult to translate.

Questioner: In Sanskrit?

Gurudev: In Sanskrit.

Questioner: What is it?

Gurudev: It is as if addressed to Shiva, but Shiva here is not the god Shiva—it is the Absolute Itself. How does it begin?

Disciple: *Ātmā Tvam* . . .

Gurudev: Ah! *Ātmā tvam, Girijā matih—Ātmā tvam Girijā matih; sahacharāh prānāh, sharīram griham; pūjā te, vishayopabhogarachanā, nidrā samādhisthitih; sanchārah padayoh pradakshinavidhih* (Wherever I walk,

31

I am going round You). *Sanchārah padayoh pradakshina-vidhih, stotrāni sarvā giro* (Whatever I utter are songs . . . hymns in praise of You).

Yadyatkarma karomi (Whatever I do), *tattadakhilam* (all that) *Shambho tavārādhanam* (is a worship to You).

This is Shankara's verse. So what is left in life, if this is life? Really, without your knowing you are doing this, you are trying to achieve this level—to see this. And if that is so, where is the veil? Where is the identification?

Questioner: Gurudev, is there a danger in that the more advantageously placed people would find excuses to oppress the Harijans and the lower castes and the poorer people, on the ground that it is their *karma* for which they are suffering?

Gurudev: No. Though I said it is their *karma* that is responsible, that does not mean: "Oh, it is their *karma*, so I can do . . ." That is not right. As far as the person who does it is concerned, he must adopt good—he must do good things. Not to oppress other people. That he must not do. Of course, the truth is there that these *karmas* are also there. What about his cruelty? This will also leave residues in him which he may have to suffer later. So, in that way, anybody living this life must adopt only good actions or good deeds. If possible, help others. Lessen your ego. Because, if others are less advantageously placed, that does not mean that you can take advantage of

32

it. There you are only nourishing your ego. That must not be done. You have to have compassion, love for human beings, your . . . friend. You must not forget the fact that in him also there is this light one day which he will reach. If you can see that, there is no reason why you can oppress him. The same light is there throughout. How can you afford to do harm to him? It is impossible; that must not be done in any case.

Questioner: Then the only aim and meaning of life is Self-realisation?

Gurudev: But is it not, when you examine it? Don't you see that that *is*—it is not because I say that. When you examine it, you see that it is the one thing you wish in life. Come on, take any example, and examine. You will see that you don't want anything else. Anything else you dislike, other than this Reality.

Questioner: If a man is seeking to be famous, in what way is that Spiritual?

Gurudev: But there is that sense of greatness in him. He is trying to work out in different ways to achieve this greatness. It is in you, effulgent.

Questioner: Can it be attained or reached without the help of a Guru?

Gurudev: No, that is not easy. That is not possible, to be very brief and open.

Questioner: Could Gurudev explain why a Guru is needed?

Gurudev: Because you have to transcend, get beyond the level of this identification. And in the process of your work there is a possibility that you get entangled again. And there, at that point, if there is somebody to help you, who has reached beyond that level, to put you There—that helps. There is one story. It is a good example: Once eleven people tried to cross a river. And after they reached the opposite bank, each one of them wanted to ascertain whether all of them were alive. Each one began to count, and each one found only ten. So all thought that one had died. Then a twelfth man comes and asks them to include the man who counted also in the group. And all the eleven were alive. This mistake takes place when you forget Yourself. You keep yourself apart from the rest of the world of objects. But this is also part of it. Whatever is seen is object. What is beyond is the Reality, the real Self which is forgotten for the time being, because you wrongly take it that you are this. Is it enough?

Questioner: May I? When the Guru speaks and the Higher Reason is awakened, somebody says there is a peace and happiness that one experiences. That type of happiness, I would like to have on a more permanent basis.

Gurudev: It is permanent. That permanence is your real Self itself. That happiness . . .

Questioner: But I want to have the feeling all the time.

Gurudev: But you cannot get that feeling when you . . . At that moment you do not connect any object with it, and you reach that peace. But in the ordinary level of happiness you connect some object with it, and you think that it is through that object you got this. But really, it is not. No object can contain the happiness. Not even your mind. When the desired object is got, the restlessness which it had when you are desiring the object stops. And then you are able to take note of your real Nature which is Happiness itself. It is always. It is permanent. And if you can see that . . . You have to *live* what you understand, what you see, and *then,* it is permanent. It is always. It is not for a short time only. But when you *think* that you got it from the object, then you seek again another object. A second time another object, a third time another object. You go on hunting after objects. There is no end to that, till at last you will come to a sense of incongruity in this way of life. And there you turn to the right direction, the real search and the real seeking. You are able to get the Guru also as a part of this seeking. It is your work itself. It is not that He wants to come and impose things on you. It is your search, and you meet the Guru. It is almost . . .

Your search and His wanting to help you, they are one. As I said this morning, that is one world.

Questioner: That happiness is the same, whether I get it from a desired object or when He takes me there through His word?

Gurudev: I will show you what it is, that is all. That is what you call, in another language, "taking you there." I remove the block. That is all. And you are there. You are not to travel far. It is there.

Questioner: The word *Guru* comes in the Vedas. When does it first come, *Guru?*

Gurudev: *Guru* literally means . . . "Gu" stands for darkness, "ru" its removal. One who removes darkness or ignorance is what you call the Guru. "From whomsoever you get enlightened, He is your Guru."

Questioner: The word comes in the Vedas?

Gurudev: Yes, it is in there. There is a verse in . . . I don't remember the verse. Does anybody? Do you know that verse?

'Gu' kārashcha . . .
'ru' kārastannirodhakrit
andhakāravināshitvād
'gurur' ityabhidhīyate

36

This is from *Guru Gītā*—what I have quoted. I do not remember the exact verse. But something like that, it goes. Our tradition is always to respect something great, even in the lower plane of phenomenal life. According to our ancient tradition, we respect our Gurus. Because it is not merely the personality that comes there. It is what we learn from Him. We respect that, and the respect we have for that subject is shown to the man who is teaching us. It is natural. And the Guru who shows the Highest or the Absolute stands for the Absolute, because the Absolute cannot be shown by anybody else. That is what I told you. He talks to you or shows you from a certain level, through the *Vidyā* aspect or the active principle functioning there, and takes you to the passive where the passive and the active, neither of them are there. And there the seeker gets the real Experience. Only the Guru who has reached that level can do that. And there, the Guru and the disciple are also absent. It is pure Experience. But once you come down to the dual plane, yes, there is that. That is necessary also to maintain this, this permanence that you are asking. This is the only dual relationship which establishes you in the non-dual. Truth is unity. It cannot be shown by anything else or any personality. The Guru stands for the Truth itself. Love reaching this Guru reaches the ultimate Love, real Love, which is unity. It is here that you realise the real Love. "The unconditioned Love towards one's own Guru is the ladder to the goal of Truth."

Questioner: Can this relationship be . . . ? Can there be a sense of dependence?

Gurudev: How can there be a dependence, a depending on something? Here, Guru stands for what?

Questioner: The Truth.

Gurudev: Can you say it is a dependence? The more you depend, the more you become independent. Nowhere else can you be like that.

Questioner: It is very difficult to understand how there can be Truth which is beyond all and at the same time something that one can have a relationship with in the phenomenal world, with the Guru . . .

Gurudev: I did not follow.

Questioner: It is difficult to understand how the Truth . . . the Guru must not be separate from the Truth, if He is to make one understand that.

Gurudev: But is it possible? Do you understand?

Questioner: Yes.

Gurudev: Then is it difficult to understand?

Questioner: No, it is difficult to understand . . .

Gurudev: But you understand the Truth . . .

Questioner: . . . the Truth.

Gurudev: . . . as shown by somebody—or the Guru, you call it. And you understand it. Then how do you say that it is difficult to understand?

Questioner: How there can be such a being?

Gurudev: How can there be such a being? From time immemorial it is like that. It *is* like that. But if you want to classify this relationship according to the ordinary level it may be difficult. It is a mysterious thing, in that level. Otherwise it is never mysterious. It is the one thing which is very clear. When you see that in a lower plane, it is mysterious. But in that plane it is the most clear thing. Clearer than anything else. For the knowledge of anything else is not the real Knowledge.

Questioner: Earlier it was mentioned about Tyagaraja, that he rose high through his music. Is that enough? Did he reach the Highest or will he have again to come back and finish?

Gurudev: If he reaches the Highest, there is no coming back. Once you reach the Absolute, it is for you to live it. And where is the coming back? To the ignorance?

Questioner: But in this . . . I was speaking about an individual who rose through music . . .

Gurudev: Yes, and if he is at the proper level, where is the coming back? It is not *going* there. Only if you *go* there, you have to come back. But you are not going there. What is blocking your real position is removed, and you are permanently there. And that is what you have to do also. It is not for a short time that you have to see that.

Questioner: But how can one do that through music, though?

Gurudev: Music takes you to that: the Absolute, *Nāda Brahma*. This morning I said that. Through *Nāda* you can be taken to a level of silent music. What is that? It is the Absolute itself. And one who has developed the music to that level can experience that, if properly guided. Same is the case with any art. And in fact all art is based on this. As far as India is concerned, all the culture, the whole culture, the whole art is based on this, when rightly . . . followed.

Questioner: *Kalā?*

Gurudev: Yes. *Kalā.*

Questioner: What is the . . . ?

Gurudev: "Ka" refers to *Brahma*, that peace that helps you to this. That is the real basis of any *kalā* or art. Indian art. Any art is so. It is like that.

Questioner: "Ka?"

Gurudev: The *Brahma*. The word refers to that *Brahma*. That "ka" has that meaning also there.

Questioner: Can one reach a sort of ecstasy? Can one . . . ?

Gurudev: Ah yes, but that is not enough.

Questioner: Even that has to be . . .

Gurudev: No, that is not enough.

Questioner: . . . transcended?

Gurudev: You have to transcend the ecstasy level also. When you follow the devotional path, it is possible to reach that ecstasy but you cannot get stuck up there. You have to transcend that level and get to that level of peace that is the Reality.

Questioner: All the Indian arts are based on Spiritual themes?

Gurudev: Yes.

Questioner: Is that an unconscious attempt to reach the Highest?

Gurudev: Conscious also. People said this not unconsciously. It is based on that *kalā*. How is it said that they know it fully that they lead you only to that? But how many people have reached through that—that is another question.

Questioner: When the great Indian epics were written, that was a conscious attempt to reach?

Gurudev: It is a conscious attempt to present the conscious attempt. Of course, that—it is Vyasa who has written that and the translator also—our Kerala translator and poet, Ezhuthachan—he was also a realised man. The active principle and the passive principle about which I told you this morning: in the *Rāmāyana*, Rama stands for the passive, Sita, the active. And it is through Sita, it is said, that you reach the Rama. But it is not a man and a woman there. It is the active principle and the passive principle. That is what is said there. And even if you take the *Mahābhārata*, if you take the whole life of Krishna, you can see that He is the living Truth itself. He is . . . the Truth itself is shown by His life. He is everywhere and nowhere. Without Him, has anything taken place in the *Mahābhārata* story? No. But nowhere He was as an individual. He was a charioteer. He was a ruler, a good warrior, good musician, good politician—what not? But at the same time He did not claim any of these things, no. Without Him nothing was achieved during His time. That shows: "Without Me, nothing is." "Me" means the Reality.

Questioner: I think calling Rama the passive principle, and Sita the active, may need further explanation.

Gurudev: Active principle—that is in the beginning of *Rāmāyana*. It is said also like that. The passive is . . . it is through that that Sita . . . I know only the Malayalam version of it:

Satchidānandam ēkam advayam parabrahmam
Nischalam sarvōpādhi nirmuktam sattāmātram
Nischayicharinyu koodātoru vasthuvennu
Nischayichālumullil Sri Rāma devanē nee.

Sita is initiating this to Hanuman who is supposed to be the devotee, and according to the direction of Rama, Sita does this. Like this, she comes down describing Rama, and then, *Ennude Tatwam,* I will tell you *My Truth*:

Ennude tatwamini cholleedāmullavannam
Ninnōdu nyān tān moolaprakriti āyatedo
Ennude Patiyāya paramātmāvu tante
Sannidhi mātram kondu nyāniva srishtikkunnu
Tal sānnidhyam kondennāl srishtamāmiva ellām
Tal svarūpattinkalākkīdunnabudha janam.

Again she comes down and she says:

Yājyanām Nārāyanan bhakti ullavarku sā-
yūjyamām mokshatte nalkeedinān niranjanan
ēvamādikalāya karmangal tante Māya-
Dēviyām enne kondu cheyyippikkunnu noonam.

"Everything is done by me," and He remains quiet there. So that is the passive principle. The active portion of the whole work is done as if by Sita. It is not by a woman, or a man, but it is the active principle and the passive principle.

Questioner: Just a minute ago something about Krishna's life was mentioned. There, when just before the big battle, Arjuna is afraid to fight. In a way is it not like being afraid to go in . . . ?

Gurudev: Yes. But what he says is: "No, I don't want to kill my kin. It is a sin. Why should I want the country? I will go and do penance in the forest." But it is not true. Really, when he saw the veterans on the opposite side, he felt cowardly. He felt he was afraid. And it is at that point that Krishna initiates *Gītā* to Arjuna. And it is also symbolic that Krishna is the charioteer and Arjuna does the fighting. Really, Krishna and Arjuna were born as Nara-Narayana. That means man and God. So man does that, and without the help of *this* charioteer, the God part, it is difficult to win. Really, the battle symbolically means *kurukshetra*: the world created by you. And the life in it is, after all, the battle in Kurukshetra. And if you can have a charioteer like this, life becomes easy.

Questioner: Even after Krishna has explained to him, it is still difficult for him to fight?

Gurudev: Yes, but he did it. Krishna was there. He did not leave him there.

Questioner: Earlier it was said that meeting the Guru is part of one's search. It seems that without even knowing one was searching, one was fortunate enough to meet . . .

Gurudev: But in spite of you, the search might have been going on. There are cases of seeing the Guru even in dream before—before meeting actually in the physical form—and not knowing who He was. Later, when he meets the Guru it is then that he realises that: "I saw Him in the dream." So, it is a part of the search. It goes on in spite of you. But consciously also he will seek. Generally, that also happens. Now that is what is generally taking place. When that urge is strong, you will knowingly seek the Guru and find Him.

Questioner: If before meeting the Guru one has already felt a strong protection, was that already the Guru?

Gurudev: Yes, it can be. Because inwardly that is going on. You are not seeing all what is inside you. As I told you, that work is going on. And when you meet Him, there you find: "Ah yes, this is what I sought." To quote my Father's example also. He had a brilliant mind. He was approaching all the people with His questions. He could not get a satisfactory answer. And He was worried very much. How to find the proper man? And in His earlier days, when He was a young boy of ten, some *siddha* had initiated Him with a *mantra*. But the *siddha* was a man who had some powers. He came to know that his early boy disciple was suffering a lot. He came to the spot where . . . My Father then was a police officer. And he came only to console Him: "Don't worry, You are going to get the proper Guru within a week." And it is within this week that He got. And from where? His Guru came all the way from Almora, to meet *only* My Father. He had four other disciples who were *sanyāsins*. What He told them before He started was, "I am going to Travancore"—then this part was Travancore—"A devotee is calling Me and I don't know when I am going to return." Being a Yogin as well, He could hear the genuine call. He said that to them and He came to meet Him. They met in a vacant house, and the questions were put to Him. And the perfect answers came, with all humility. And immediately, like a flash, He remembered what the earlier *kārya guru* told him—he can be said to be the *kārya guru*, the man who initiated Him earlier. And then He asked for the help. And only when He asked for the help, the Guru said: "I came here *only for this*." Till He asked for it, He did not say. So a real Guru will never impose. It is a clear example.

Questioner: When we think of the great religious leaders, the problem that comes to mind is that the message of the Guru reaches such few people, and here is our country of six hundred and fifty million. How to get the message to them?

Gurudev: But even if you give the message, if they are not ready to receive that, how is it to be useful? It can

46

reach them, but it will be properly received only when the person is ready for it. That is why I said real seeking is necessary before it can be conveyed. Otherwise it will pass over the head, and they don't want it. What is the use of Spirituality? You want something—you want to live, earn money, and become famous—something like that. It is all phenomenal, in the ordinary level. But the *real* value of it will be recognised only by the real seeker. That is always, in the world's history, a minority. Just as the real Gurus are also a minority. I mean *Kārana Guru*. One who can take you to the Highest, to the Absolute. They are always, in any period of time, a minority.

Questioner: Sri Shankaracharya has argued in favour of becoming a *sanyāsin*. He said it is necessary.

Gurudev: Yes, their idea . . . I have to mention this in connection with my Father also. I told you, my Father's Guru was a *sanyāsin*. The other four disciples were also *sanyāsins*. But He did not allow my Father to become a *sanyāsin*. And He is the only person who was allowed to . . . whom the Guru asked to accept disciples. That means, *sanyāsa* is not always necessary to realise the Truth. But according to the time, each teacher, or the Guru, or *āchāryas* model their teaching. Then the *sanyāsa* might have been necessary. But we have had so many Gurus who were not *sanyāsins*. What about . . . *Tat Tvam Asi* itself was initiated by a father to his son. And in the *Gītā*, before the salutation to the

Guru, till Shankaracharya it comes down from father to son. It starts, the verse starts:

Nārāyanam Padmabhuvam Vasishtam
Shaktim ca tatputra Parāsharam ca
Vyāsam Shukam Gaudapadam mahāntam
Govindayogīndramathāsya shishyam
Srī Sankarāchārya . . .

Till then, the lineage comes down from father to son. At a certain period of time, whatever is necessary the teachers adopt, or the *āchāryas* adopt. In the *shāstras* it is described: the householder and the *sanyāsi* Gurus. Both are described. If Truth is in spite of anything, a genuine urge is all that is required. Here and now, if you can open your eyes, you are at the right place.

As I quoted earlier, that verse, *Ātmā tvam* . . . We don't want to destroy anything. You just open your eyes and see the Truth, that is all. We don't want to destroy the world. It is only to show the Truth. What is there to be destroyed? What is there to be renounced? He who renounced also has to be renounced. The whole life becomes a meditation, and it only helps you towards That. What helps you, should you renounce that? If taken in the proper perspective, anything is only to help you. Krishna Himself was urging Arjuna to act: *Nimitta mātram bhava Savyasāchin* ("You be only My instrument in the fight") . . .

Questioner: If one looks at things that way, then one does not need to view the world as *māyā* or illusion?

Gurudev: No, we don't take into consideration *māyā* at all in our discussion. Everything can be explained. Then why *māyā*? It is not necessary. *Māyā* is something that cannot be explained. It is not necessary. *Māyā* has no beginning. That is what is said about *māyā*: it has no beginning, but there is an end. What is that . . . what does that mean? But we know everything shows only the Truth, Consciousness, or Bliss. And the whole life is a *pūjā* to That, or a worship to That. Then, what is there to be given up? There is no question of *māyā*.

Questioner: Are not some things more helpful to Spiritual growth than others? Some actions, some atmospheres more helpful for Spiritual development?

Gurudev: In the beginning, yes, you adopt that. Such things—environment, atmosphere—that is always helpful. That you need, for your work. Even for worship, why do you want to go to a temple, or a place of worship? Christians go to the churches, Hindus go to the temples, like that. So that environment helps you to raise your thoughts and feelings.

Questioner: What is the way to maintain that atmosphere in any kind of environment?

Gurudev: Once you have become quite used to this,

wherever you are, you will be able to bring up that atmosphere. You must get used to that.

Questioner: So the fact that it is said that the entire life is a worship, is that a license to . . . ?

Gurudev: Do anything? Do *anything?* No. You do only the right thing. Once you see This, it is This that guides you. Not, "Doing anything." That is not the attraction. It is *This.* So, how can you go to bad ways? Bad ways means that which takes you away from This. And good is that which takes you . . . takes you Here. And how can you adopt the bad ways when this is your aim? That question is: "Oh, I can do anything." If it is only a worship, you can do anything. No, that will not happen. Doing anything is not the aim. That is the aim: the Reality.

Questioner: Gurudev said one need not give up anything from the world we like, but that does not mean one should not . . . turn the whole life . . .

Gurudev: There are two words: "need not" and "should not." (Laughter) When you say you "need not," . . . in the beginning you have to adopt certain things. It is not said, "should not." When you say "should not," you are in the object world. When you say you "need not," you are in the Spiritual. That is the difference. Whatever is not favourable, you may give up in the beginning. And later the whole obstacle . . . even the obstacles become means. So there are no more obstacles later.

Questioner: Can one change one's *karma*? Is it possible? You are born with a certain *karma*, it is said, but can . . . ?

Gurudev: Yes, in human beings compared with animals, there are two faculties: discrimination and free will. It is because of these two qualities that man can change his *karmas*, and reach the Absolute. These help. It is generally said that only man—human beings—can realise. That is because compared with animals, these two qualities are there. And by the use of these faculties you can change your *karma*. Apart from that, the attention in this direction itself can change the *karmas*. And that is what is taking place also. When you have a bad period, when the astrologer says, "Oh, you have a bad period," he prescribes certain medicines or certain ways. He goes and does that. It is because you have these faculties in you that you are able to do that. You are making use of this. And by the use of these two, free will and discrimination, you can change *karmas*. Otherwise what is the hope of mankind? A set of *karmas* will produce another set of *karmas*, and they will produce another set of *karmas*: it goes on indefinitely. There is no end to all this. But when are you going to see the Truth, the Reality?

Questioner: Even while one is working in the Spiritual, is one creating *samskāras* which . . . ?

Gurudev: Yes, as long as you are a doer . . . doing action with the doership, you are creating *samskāras*.

Questioner: But how does one get beyond that?

Gurudev: But your work is there, higher still. And then once you see that there is no doer there, once you see that permanently, *samskāras* stop.

Questioner: Permanently. But in the meantime?

Gurudev: In the meantime, your aim is that and you are working towards that.

Questioner: So they will affect you less than if . . . just like an ordinary . . .

Gurudev: Yes.

Questioner: Can one do an action and at the same time, can there be no doer?

Gurudev: Yes. You know the Realised Man's life is described in *Jnāna Vāsishta:*

> *Dehābhimāne galite vijnāte paramātmani*
> *Yatra yatra mano yāti, tatra tatra samādhayah.*
> (Wherever the mind travels, He is enjoying *samādhi*).

Where is the doer there? He is also living in the world. "Whether there is thought or not, to be always self-centred is called the natural state (*Sahaja-samādhi*)."

(*Ātmā Nirvriti*) Rama was ruling the country, Janaka was ruling the country, Krishna was doing all these activities. Was there any doer there? There are three kinds of, say, Realised Men in this world. One who gives more importance to the *samādhis*. Another who gives more importance to *viveka,* reading scriptures, interpreting and like that, always. But there is a third, *vyavahāra,* who is always in the level of activities. He shows and lives the Truth through his actions.

EVENING TALK

Questioner: Is meeting the Guru an accident?

Gurudev: It is never an accident. Meeting the Guru is never an accident. My Father's case is a clear example for that. As I said earlier, He was approaching each and every Spiritual man He could possibly meet and putting His questions there, and He was not in a position to get a clear answer, at least not a satisfactory answer. And then when He was worrying like this, not being able to find a proper Guru, there was His *kārya guru,* who had some powers, who had initiated Him with a *mantra* when He was only ten years old. He came to know that his early disciple was worrying, and he came to the spot and told Him, "You are going to meet the proper Guru within a week." And though in the course of His work He might have forgotten this, one day—then His work was in the court as a prosecuting inspector—when He was coming out of the court, He saw a *sanyāsin* seated on the parapet wall on the side of the road. Seeing Him, this man got up and came near Him and just after preliminary . . . acquaintance He asked Him, the *sanyāsin* asked Him, "Can we walk for a mile?" "Yes." And They walked and entered into a vacant building. It appeared as if He knew the whole place. And They sat there for the whole night, He Himself asking the questions and the Guru, the *sanyāsin,* answering in the most perfect manner, with all humility. This struck Him. And immediately, like a flash, He remembered what His *kārya guru* had told Him. He asked Him the instruction, His Spiritual instruction, and it was there it started. And then He said, "It is only for *this* that I came."

Now, do you know wherefrom He came? He came from Almora, from North India. And there also He was telling His other disciples, "A devotee in Travancore is calling me, and I am going there. I don't know when I am returning." And so, you see, He knew this from there. He came to Him. Can this be an accident? Though outwardly it may appear to my Father, from outside, as an accident, it is never an accident. And that was how He met His Guru. And His Guru was a Yogin. He could see through the minds and all that. Yogin—and Jnanin, too. My Father also had reached such a position that He could contact His Guru in the subtle and He could contact Him whenever He wanted, so that instructions are given and followed like this.

Questioner: In view of the importance of the Guru for a person to achieve Self-realisation, a question that comes to mind is: how a Guru comes to take His place. For instance, how did Your revered Father come to be a Guru, or how did You come to be a Guru? That is the question which seekers of the Truth, anxious to find a Guru, want to know.

Gurudev: My Father's Guru was a *sanyāsin* and He had, apart from my Father, four other disciples. All of them were *sanyāsins*. Though they had come to the right point, right level of Experience, to none of them He gave the permission to accept disciples. My Father was not asked to take up *sanyāsa*. He was asked to remain as a householder. At the same time He was the person to whom He gave the permission to accept the disciples. And that was how He started accepting them.

But even to come to some detail. He had His vision of the Guru whenever He wanted. And each time, in the early periods, whenever somebody approached Him for this, He would ask His permission: "Can I accept?" But He would answer, "I have already given you permission, then why do you each time want to ask me about that? You can accept." So generally, the disciple, even though he is permitted to accept disciples, will accept only after the Guru's leaving the body. Not when the Guru is alive . . .

The Realisation part, it is not possible to transfer. The other aspects of the Guru, generally, can be transferred. That is what has happened in many cases. For example, Ramakrishna Paramahamsa: what I have heard about it is that He transferred that power to Vivekananda, his main disciple, to continue the work. It need not be always through nomination.

And there was one Tatwaraya who was a very great devotee of his Guru. But he got stuck up in the level of . . . he was a bit *samādhi*-minded. But the Guru knew that that was not enough. He had to get beyond that. He tried His level best to get him out of that. But it was impossible. So He adopted the cruellest method possible for a devoted disciple. But that also, it was a sacrifice on His part, because he was so loving, so devoted to Him. But He adopted that way. There was a practice in that *āshram* that on full moon day the Guru did not use oil for His bath. He purposefully asked Tatwaraya to bring some oil for His bath. Then he innocently thought, "Perhaps the Guru might have forgotten that this is the full moon day." He almost . . . he was almost on the point of reminding Him of the day. Then He flared up and got very angry at him and asked him, "You are reminding me of full moon? You don't . . . you cannot see the position of your Guru even? Don't you know my life is beyond time and space? And you are reminding me of full moon!

58

You are not worthy to be my disciple. Get out of my sight."

What can you do? He could not say anything. He was drifting like that, and he went out. And to where? He could not know, did not know. And then the Guru called some other disciples and asked them to follow him: "He will be going straight to the sea, and after he has got in a few steps, hold him from behind and tell him that the Guru wants him." And that Guru's—oh, there are jealousies everywhere—those disciples also were a bit jealous. So when they heard the first order, they were a bit happy. But this order also was given to them, so they followed. And accordingly, according to the Guru's instructions, when he stepped into the sea, they pulled him from behind and told him that the Guru wants him back. There also, he could not understand. He came back singing the *kīrtanams*—songs in praise of the Guru—because he was such a devoted disciple. He came, and fell at His feet. The Guru's. In that pose He transfers His powers to the disciple. And in that pose He leaves the body.

Tatwaraya is a famous name, in South India at least, and the story about himself and his Guru. So there are stories like that, generally. Many other stories can be quoted like this. Generally the Guru's . . . that aspect of it can be transferred. But not the Realisation part. Realisation he has to reach by work. Of course, the Guru's Grace will be there throughout.

Also available through Advaita Publishers:

ATMA DARSHAN
(At the Ultimate)
by Sri Krishna Menon (Sri Atmananda)

ATMA NIRVRITI
(Freedom and Felicity in the Self)
by Sri Krishna Menon (Sri Atmananda)

ATMANANDA TATTWA SAMHITA
(Recorded Talks of Sri Atmananda)
Compiled, edited, and
Malayalam portions translated by
Sri K. Padmanabha Menon (Sri Adwayananda)